Kháos

A Collection of Poems

Mulotong T Jamir

BookLeaf Publishing

India | USA | UK

Made with ❤ on the BookLeaf Publishing Platform
www.bookleafpub.in
www.bookleafpub.com

Dedication

To the people who are fragments of this route. A past forgiven, a present written, and an unseen future we must hope for. To the distant who seek a solace, not found in the horizon. To the hopeless and the proud. To the rich in heart, and to the poor in heart. To the deceived, and to the saved. To the sheep who hear his voice, to the ones who are yet to come. May his grace reach and save us all.

Preface

When I first began to work on this book, my goal was and has always been the same. To take the readers on a journey. Whatever elements it may be, I simply love diving into the vast pool of various genres and topics. To express my work either through stories, poems, free writings. I just like expressing my creations in all artistic approach. For this book, "Kháos" I have strictly restricted myself to indulge into the world of poetry. Experimenting, as well as crafting my own art in this collection of poems. Playing around with the identity of mystery and, overall a sense of the rather dark truth and at the same time, finding the joy amid the "Kháos".

Acknowledgements

I would like to express my heartfelt gratitude to all the readers who took the time to go through my work. Also, all this would not have been possible without he who died for me. John 3:16.

Flower

The queen of yesterday,
Her might and aura in display.
Homes garnered and trampled;
Under her feet, shackled.

Born not of noble blood but, meek;
In a little house, indeed a clique.
Her eyes roared of fiery ambition,
Until the heart grew cold in submission.

Who can rival her wisdom?
A vicious tongue sheathed in her thumb.
Can any mortal stand his ground?
When even her own lover is earthbound.

A throne blessed in glory,
Only to be abused poorly.
Sons and daughter snatched away!
Has her conscience led her astray?

The queen of yesterday!
May she steadfast before delay!
Forsaken in her solitary chamber,
A cold heart, the kingdom remembers.

Fleeting Time

A sea of glass, alluring in sight;
Mayhap chiselled from lapis and white;
The master covets, in just and right.

The ship steers onwards with the breeze,
Through the sands of time and memories.
Painting the tempter from the eyes of Eve.

Truly, the sails await no one;
The sweet melody, not from heaven;
A storm brews from the dragon's drum.

Brave and melancholic stirred men;
Some had fallen deep in slumber again,
Alas! The salt of the sea has made their den.

Now! Little ones of poor in spirit!
See them dressed in angelic merit,
Unlike the greedy, who were demented.

Oblivion Wolf

A crown decorated of snapdragons;
Commend, adorned with flattery;
Wealth, selfishly plucked in glee.

A bewitching hearty smile of tranquillity,
Tenderly moulded towards sympathy,
Oh! How blinded by her own treachery.

A favourite amongst the chosen crowd,
Her compassion leaves none in doubt!
Yet, a whisper enough to set her aroused.

A heel firmly planted on sacred ground,
And the other, seeded on lustful bound,
Her nightly deeds are indeed pronounced.

A false testimony wooed over the youth;
The ferocious lips! Quick to immoral truth,
From the bed of a stranger, she fumed.

A Silent Letter

The sacrilege maiden of the rock;
Imparted a prestige, not of Nimrod.
Lonely alone in the cradle of silk;
Such was birth, is it all destined?

From the bed, cries out a soul;
A river of tears, who can make thou whole?
The silent trails and battles wages,
How long until tended by angels.

Cuts and bruises martyred,
Yet not enough to be bothered.
Pills and miasma, the eyes gazes on;
Will this tragedy finally be sought upon.

Spring and autumn bids adieu;
Thieves and lions are forever renewed.
The harsh winter comforts no more,
May summer bring about a nevermore.

A word offered amidst the rain;
It calms and soothes my soul from shame.
Faithful and loving, who doesn't chastise.
A precious friend worth gold, where can I find?

The Story of Self-Love

Life is a dream, unrealised till end;
The truth seen, before the final rest;
Idols and fraudulence, all must bend.

A mind of eternity, desperate for utopia;
Ambitions and wistful conquests,
The sickness began with an idea.

Eden! Pure from unknown blemish,
Two cups! Two tables! Not a myth!
Who was it, who rejected the prince?

A river of honey and joyful sunrise;
In fact, a paradise beyond paradise,
Free from dirt, yet came about our demise.

History engraved in cold blood;
A chaotic race, ended in a flood;
Ignorant still, each prey in worship.

Rebirthing

Of smiles and weary hearts;
A man of faith heals, where he walks.
Stranded from the gaze of the world;
Do a good deed, hidden from pearled.

Cast off the strings of deceit,
For this crooked path bores defeat.
Alas! The one who stands alone!
Who can aid thou when condoned.

The immaculate unison of grace,
Wash clean! Are thou not in this race?
For the days are corrupted and evil;
Come forth! Before the hour of retrieval.

Amid the chaos, this light shines bright;
Gathering the lost and the broken in sight.
Do away the former acts of the past,
Before the King has his judgement passed.

The Fallacious Owl

Drunk in the labour of blood and tears;
Jaspers and rubies bathe in frankincense.
Feasting upon the spines of the poor;
March forth! They hoist the flag of grandeur.

Wondrous paradox of greed and desire;
So bold in secret! wears the helm of a liar.
Forged and dipped in a coat of velvet;
Savouring the bread of the tormented.

A chalice worthy of the seat of honour;
Loins and garments stripped for the lover.
Selflessly offering one's purity on a platter;
To gain fame and wealth, does it truly matter?

Radiant warriors and knights of valour;
Thy armour lies frozen without a master.
Has all fled this scene of glory and power?
Truly, a haughty tongue is quick to danger.

Mighty oak of viridescent and cherry;
Pours a shade for the hopeless merry.
Fiends and ghouls feed off the fruits;
A sheep's hide! caring not for the roots.

The Girl with The Diamond Eye

The girl with the diamond eye,
Stalks the pestilence in the night.
Sacred fire draped by her umbrella;
Black fit checked, like a gangsta.

Little boy tossing around in bed,
The vengeful fangs await his death.
A predator hiding behind blinds;
Lassie was swift to have it sliced.

Buzzed and flushed! The uncles were;
Just right behind, the reaper dwelled.
The girl with the diamond eye,
Huffed and puffed! But never terrified.

Uplifting the shade under her right,
She drove her brolly through the blight.
Breaking out her trusty hoover,
Inky sneakers trampled the monster.

The girl with the diamond eye,
Who tiptoes into the brilliant sky.
Keeping safe the lone and frightened,
From the filthy nails of the tyrant.

Three Ugly Sirens

Three ugly sirens,
Your mouth drools like a lion!
A shuffle of fancy dresses;
How long until one confesses?

Sneaking into the Hosp house;
Clothed in sand, quick to sellout.
Kissing the wounds of forlorn,
Disgust basked in their scorns.

Three ugly sirens!
Hide your true intentions!
Blasting triumphant tears,
Ah! Be haunted by nightmares!

Skin and bones, vessel lone;
Wretched witch, may you atone.
The dead will testify one day,
Steel oneself! Kneel and pray.

Three ugly sirens!
Purge the cries of the demons!
Yet your actions births perplex,
Let his sword be drawn on your necks.

Unrelenting Hope

The journey is vast, tho' conquered;
By the one invisible one, treasured.
Shackled and burdened, not for long;
This passing wind, face it headstrong.

Rejoice in the change of season!
Do not lose heart, you were chosen.
Chains of yesterday, begone from sight!
Mighty soldier! Take up the good fight!

Closed doors, never a cry unheard;
Surrender thy yolk, and be cured.
Wail not for the shameful flory;
Celebrate in lieu, the future glory.

The beast's carcass, rots to nothingness;
Like the lips of a mocker, ever so changes.
Who so benefits from such a quarrel?
Let the prideful drown! Up from their castle.

Pour in me, a pure heart today;
Shower me with love and grace this day.
The one true son! Be my rock;
Deliver me! From what I cannot.

A Lypiménos Tale

A man destined for great honour;
Unseen thrones laid in his favour.
Oh! How the beliefs were reckoning;
Ruination struck! From his house spring.

The man sways his bitter heart away;
Reminiscing the brilliance, a lost hurray.
Out from his window, he yearned the flair;
The joy of youth, snatched without a spare.

Galloping on his horse, he fled the scene;
Up on his only friend, who never schemed.
Befuddled and drunk in the motherly tavern;
The shoving of poison, down his cavern.

Vile moon in wait, his conscience burnt;
A demonic slumber, he tossed and turned.
Naked deceivers' dances to his essence,
Enraged! Who is to blame for this sentence.

Cursing off the night and the day;
The man once destined, ran out astray.
From the walls of a home, a stallion cries;
Loyal to his master, who never said goodbye.

Inori

A mournful twisted garden,
Where hate is born without pardon.
Love and mercy grew distant,
When everyone's heart stiffened.

Lust overcame the joy of beauty,
Thirsty hounds yearning for the body.
Is the thrill of romance forgotten?
Materialism has it made a burden.

For all the wrongful reasons,
We celebrate life in treason.
Though people are in bondages,
A hope lingered through the ages.

An exceeding compassion ushers;
Yet, we find ways to hate each other.
Broken families, broken homes;
Plotting a demise rather than condone.

Under the faces we bear open;
A hug longed for, unspoken.
Fighting a futile war amongst us;
Ignoring the sorrowful illness.

Providence

I do the things I do not want to,
Though I know they serve of no virtue;
I still do it, for it is my nature to do so.

By birth, I am but a shattered cymbal;
Non-existent, a mockery for the cynical;
But again, kept alive for repentance.

I wonder if not for this broken chastity;
To strike me down this instant for blasphemy;
But is his patience so easy to exhaust?

I am ashamed, I am guilty of murder;
Dreaming of a freedom, not of liberation;
I seek blatantly for the city before creation.

Imprisoned in me, the crimson stains;
I cannot move this mountain in my days;
Even so, I sleep with this kindled faith.

Myo Sotis

I find pleasure in them no more;
Bloodied tides have reached the shore;
Imminent rapture, can none candour.

My morality drowns in the ocean;
My heart is weighed in grim,
As a consequence of sin.

My own voice is a stranger to me;
Incapable of discerning, let it be;
I live in fear; none hears my plea.

The perishable held dear in vanity;
A cruel rhapsody leaves my lips,
Before I too lose my sanity.

Forget-me-not;
The looming disaster undid its knot;
I close my eyes, adrift in this ballade.

A Dying Passion

To which authority does a writer hail?
To craft the most elaborate lie and tale.
To chisel the tender emotions of a chapter,
The paradigm of a labourer and the master.

The kind unknown to humane perception,
Drifting into the minds of pious deception.
The beauty found in the midst of calamity,
Gluttonized with wine, ripped from reality.

A shot of the high, I seek for it more!
A gamble of fate, preordained in fore.
A land infested by witches and druids,
A maiden of pain, vanquished in lucid.

The subtle knock of comfort, I find in it;
The conscience miserably yearns for it.
Till my heart cries no more for the wicked;
Let my conscious perish, to dream more vivid.

Precious darling, I remember no longer;
Her eyes were like emerald, or I wonder.
My heart is done for, I can return no more,
Only this addiction remains, this is my fall.

City of Dystopia

In this city of dystopia,
The red stirs our melancholia.
Ruling over the notion,
Vessels emptied of emotion.

Everyone walks and talks freedom,
Even though, we are held by none.
Governed by laws of men,
Men or someone else, I say again.

It is in our nature to serve,
Rebellious, blameworthy;
We escape the death, we deserve;
A tragic story it is, I can only observe.

Our lips are restless,
To preach the story of love;
To lend a shoulder to the helpless,
Faithfully, in public, never enough.

Only if the snakes were hidden;
They slither inside homes, as it is written.
But let me write a story of hypocrisy,
The blind leads the blind, surely, we agree.

The Holly Theatre

To love, is to take a knee,
And serve in righteousness;
To garnish the aroma of good deed,
Without the act of selfishness.

But a crown of pride is preferred,
Whilst, the crown of humility;
Is shattered, pricking the tongue;
Yet, a modest song is still sung.

Comforted with lies over lies,
Flagrantly done before our eyes.
Horrible beings we are,
Satisfied only after leaving a scar.

Patiently waiting in ponder,
Waiting for the next martyr;
Be it innocent or sinful,
As long as done, in good will.

This majestic ceremony,
Meaningless to the condemned;
Mostly performed so for money,
The dead will confess for this folly.

The Hummingbird

Once there was a hummingbird,
Who was an orphan since birth.
Harsh and brutish was the wind;
All he wanted, was to fit in.

Fortune favoured him however,
He wasn't alone in this endeavour.
Surrounded by fellow feathered friends,
Rallying the chirps, he could depend.

They would testify long tweets,
Often inviting the young one to greets.
Professing about the grand horizon,
He took heart, despite his condition.

The gruelling stars and the sun,
They seem like an everlasting run.
Casting off the old wings for new,
The nestling took off into the blue.

The bird was a marvel, not to all;
They began to hurl insult and lies;
Saddened but not daunted, he stood tall;
Taking the flight towards the skies.

Rue

Perhaps, time wasn't the villain;
In consequence to what,
The sentimental has it written.

For there is, a time to heal;
A time for sorrow,
Which passes on without appeal.

The trouble starts with, if only.
A buried vault,
Awoken when it pleases, likely.

Regardless, wouldn't it be better;
To taste the fruit,
Rather than to be a victim of fetter.

Where Death has no power;
Whatsoever, we can only,
Carry on this weight forever.

The Weight of Blood

The diligent knight knows not the morn,
Riding the narrow gate, even when worn.
A servant for the rich, not for the poor;
He sorrowfully cleans his helm of rigueur.

A benevolent bishop, where can I find?
Ever ready to cater the ache of the twined.
At the cost of her vigour, keen in sincerity;
Veiled by the darkness, follows a false deity.

The rook, proud and courageous in all;
She could carry the Earth, if heeded the call.
Alas! The future glory was well prepared;
Yet, the pride came to fruition, left despaired.

Now, the king was loved, rightfully so;
Not for the crown, but honesty without flaw.
Though, the inevitable destruction brewed;
After this death, the battle of egos colludes.

The pawns! Yes, the pawns hold their rank;
Restless for a promotion, equipped for a flank.
Lazy swine, glancing for the easy way out;
Shameless traitors, the assured benefit of doubt.

Deceitful Tongue

The sails waves of liberty,
The ship ramparts sturdy;
But a wheel steers its destiny.

Even the epic lion of ours,
The majestic king;
Can be mastered behind bars.

Yet who can tame the tongue?
An organ often presumed,
From the old to the young.

From this vicious serpent,
The innocent is condemned;
The ignorant are commended.

Tell me, who can tame it?
This orchestrator, a hypocrite;
What the heart is full of, it vomits.

Sans Espoir

Friendship is a chosen delight,
To be celebrated despite,
The desirous want for a bribe.

Is life, only to be remembered;
When something is to be offered.
Status and riches needed, to be heard.

The pious crowd of judgement,
Awaits either the sound moment,
Of demise or glory, never silent.

Strangers arrives to a funeral,
Reciting suitable poems of rue,
Whilst, never present in the blue.

Piteous and rebellious we are;
The perishable, treasured in a jar,
Solely to die alone without revoir.

Prince of Darkness

The struggle rest not with the flesh;
Particularly not with anyone, I confess;
But he who wears the innocent dress.

The world is evil and it always will be,
Ruled by he who decided not to knee,
Deceiving souls for a glimpse of money.

Our minds and hearts are in subject,
To the beauty and music of the wicked,
Kissing the elite heels of the twisted.

Men are born sinful but with a hope;
A free will gifted down to cast the vote,
An unceasing war, whom to devote?

Chasing after the lustful pleasures,
How long until your heart withers,
A false promise is all, from this giver.

Narcissus

Life is no more than a mist,
We live in an illusion of bliss.
Putting down righteousness,
Performing all horrid in Idleness.

Lawless city of deranged minds,
And It's hideous acts of all kinds.
Everyone does what they want,
Putting on a breastplate of vaunt.

The lust of the eyes! Deemed,
And sought as love, it seemed.
Where sulphur, chosen over hell;
Oblivious fools! All under a spell.

Double-minded helps the blind;
Loud lips are silent right on time.
Afraid of persecution from wrong;
Preaching peace before the storm.

Debauchery and prostitution,
And the so-called art in fashion;
Nudity has become the mark,
Of beauty for those in the dark.

A Dreadful Thesis

Surrounded on every side,
By the earthly and not the bride;
They dally and hope for my demise,
Because I no longer bear any ties.

Suffering in the body, and within;
Surely a reward awaits free from sin.
Chastened by the fire and water,
The tides rages but I do not falter.

Either by sheer will or by hope;
"The hope in the unseen" I quote.
How far can materialism take you?
And woe to those who are new.

Grandest tombs are forgotten,
Unmarked graves will soon open.
Storing treasures in a dying place,
We miss what is offered, his grace.

Lady in black stalks the night,
Always hungry and thirsty for a bite.
Slithering into the hearts of men,
Crawling into their dreams again.

The promised eternal life exists,
A life after death, not of this.
Not of good works whatsoever,
Aren't taxmen in the same pleasure?

Ungodly, utter ungodliness;
A warning to be in readiness.
Garnishing a departing beauty,
Many slumbers away, surely.

Awake in walking towards doom,
A cruel world, not that I assume.
All will face the first and the last;
We are at ends of this hourglass.

www.ingramcontent.com/pod-product-compliance
Lightning Source LLC
LaVergne TN
LVHW050948200726
843508LV00011B/2470